ESSenn

Accounting for
the Small Business

Time-saving books that teach specific skills to busy people, focusing on what really matters; the things that make a difference – the *essentials*.

Other books in the series include:

Business Letters that Work

Expand Your Vocabulary

Develop a Winning a Marketing Plan

Leading Teams

Making the Most of Your Time

Solving Problems

Coaching People

Hiring People

Making Great Presentations

Writing Good Reports

The Ultimate Business Plan

Writing Business E-mails

For full details please send for a free copy of the latest catalogue.
See back cover for address.

Accounting for the Small Business

Phil Stone

ESSENTIALS

Published in 2001 by
How To Books Ltd, 3 Newtec Place,
Magdalen Road, Oxford OX4 1RE, United Kingdom
Tel: (01865) 793806 Fax: (01865) 248780
e-mail: info@howtobooks.co.uk
www.howtobooks.co.uk

British Library Cataloguing in Publication Data.
A catalogue record for this book is available from
the British Library.

Edited by Francesca Mitchell
Cover design by Shireen Nathoo Design
Produced for How To Books by Deer Park Productions
Typeset by PDQ Typesetting, Newcastle-under-Lyme, Staffordshire
Printed and bound in Great Britain by Bell & Bain Ltd., Glasgow

NOTE: The material contained in this book is set out in good faith for
general guidance and no liability can be accepted for loss or expense
incurred as a result of relying in particular circumstances on
statements made in the book. Laws and regulations are complex
and liable to change, and readers should check the current position
with the relevant authorities before making personal arrangements.

ESSENTIALS *is an imprint of*
How To Books

Contents

Preface

All too often the owners of small businesses are very good at the practical aspects of running their businesses but totally inept when it comes to looking after the books. In many cases this lack of knowledge about a key area of running your business could lead to failure. By spending a small amount of time each week on looking after the books, and understanding the relevance of the figures, such failure could easily be avoided.

The question of financial controls within a business should not be left just to your accountant to provide annual figures. The business is yours and you must take responsibility for the primary preparation of financial accounts. Without the most basic of accounts you cannot possibly maintain control over your business.

A business will often run out of cash and, upon approaching the bank for assistance, will be turned down because the business is unprofitable. If steps had been taken to monitor the financial position the problem would have been recognised before it happened and corrective steps could have been taken a lot earlier.

Basic financial records are not difficult to construct and they could mean the difference between success and failure.

Phil Stone

1 What are Financial Accounts?

Business accounts should not be left to your accountant. You must be able to understand your own financial accounts.

In this chapter three things that really matter:
~ The different forms of accounts
~ Why you need accounts
~ The basic contents of accounts

The preparation of financial accounts is avoided by many business owners and merely left to their accountant. This means that they have no real control over their finances, which form a key indicator of how their business is performing.

This is not to suggest that you should never use an accountant for your accounts. You should use the specialist knowledge of your accountant for expert accountancy advice or to finalise your accounting records.

Unless you specifically employ your accountant at least on a monthly basis to prepare regular management accounts, it is crucial that you have a system in place that can give you regular reports on how your business is performing.

Without such a system, you could find that you are actually trading at a loss. When your annual accounts are subsequently shown to your bank manager in order to ask for funding you will be turned down. Your business could then fail simply because you failed to monitor your finances.*

Is this you?

Accountancy is a specialist skill, I don't have the expertise. • I pay my accountant good money, there is no reason for me to get involved. • I already keep a cash book that tells me all I need to know. • Balance sheets and profit and loss accounts are too complicated for me, I wouldn't know where to start.

* *It is your responsibility to monitor your finances and take corrective action when things go wrong. Without any accounts, by the time you discover that things have gone wrong, it is too late.*

The different forms of accounts

In general terms there are three different forms of accounts:

~ projected accounts

~ management accounts

~ annual accounts.

Most business owners have no problem with preparing projections for their business. Most of the high street banks have specialist packs available for businesses, which contain specific projection forms for completion. The layout, styling and headings are then relatively easy to understand.

The most common form of projected account is the cash flow forecast. This deals with the cash requirements of your business usually over a one year period. Whilst a cash flow forecast is a valuable management tool, it does ignore profitability and therefore its use is limited.

In some cases a projected balance sheet and profit and loss account are also prepared, but this is usually done by an accountant.

This is due, in the main, to a lack of understanding by the entrepreneur as to how they should be prepared. In some cases, even after they have been prepared, the entrepreneur is unable to explain exactly what they reveal.*

Management accounts are accounts that enable you to manage your business. In most businesses, however, such accounts are totally ignored despite their being the most important. It is these accounts that are most valuable to your business because they will reveal whether you are actually making a profit or trading at a loss.

Management accounts are usually prepared on a monthly basis and then compared with the projected accounts to assess ongoing performance. The reasons therefore that these accounts are so important is that they enable you to monitor your performance and take early corrective action if necessary.

The third form of accounts are the annual accounts. These will normally be completed by your accountant as at your year end. These

* *All too often I have interviewed clients requesting funding who have to defer to their accountant when questioned about the forecasts. This does not instil confidence. They should be able to explain the forecasts themselves. It is their business, not their accountant's.*

accounts are also important to your business, but for different reasons. The annual accounts enable you to take the specialist advice of your accountant, for example, in order to minimise your tax liability.

Your accountant will also ensure that you comply with all relevant legislation concerning your accounting records and returns, especially if you operate as a limited liability company.

Why you need accounts

Most businesses maintain a cash accounting system which, although important, is also inadequate because it does not monitor performance. It takes no account of the profits or losses that you are making. Now that we have established the three main forms of accounts, it is important that you understand their function.

Projected accounts are used to chart the finances of your business over a future defined period. They represent your plans for the future and will normally be incorporated into your business plan. They should normally be prepared by you and be based upon your historical financial performance. This will ensure that they are as realistic as possible.*

If you are a new start business then obviously you will have no historic performance on which to base your figures. Under these circumstances you should seek help from an appropriate business adviser who can offer guidance in this respect. They will have access to a number of databases which can compare your figures with other similar businesses on a ratio basis. Chapter six contains a detailed description of the use of ratio analysis.

Management accounts should be the main constituent of your management information system. They do not need to be prepared to the same level of accuracy as your annual accounts, but they do need to be accurate enough to be meaningful. They should preferably use the same major headings as those used in the accounts prepared by your accountant. This could make the preparation

It is probable that you would like to seek the advice of your accountant just to make sure that statutory payments such as VAT and National Insurance are correctly calculated.

of your annual accounts a lot easier for your accountant and therefore possibly cheaper.

The essential reason for keeping management accounts is that they can provide you with a snapshot of your finances which you can compare with your projections. This is why it is necessary to compile management accounts on at least a monthly basis. Your projections will have been calculated on a monthly basis and so can easily be compared with the management accounts.

If this is done on a monthly basis it means that a maximum of one month can pass before financial problems are identified and corrective action taken. This places you in a far stronger position to succeed in business.*

* All too often projections are placed in a drawer and no attempt is made to compare performance until the year end accounts are prepared.

As already explained, annual accounts are usually prepared to enable you to meet your legal obligations and, depending on the size of your business, may require that a full audit of your books be carried out by your accountant.

The problem with relying on the annual

accounts to monitor your business is that they are often a long way out of date. They only represent a snapshot of your business as at your year end. In addition, depending on the efficiency of your accountant, they may well be prepared six months, or even later, after your year end.

This could mean that if your business was encountering financial difficulties in the early part of your trading year, this would only come to light at least 12 months after the event. This is certainly far too late to take any corrective action.

The basic contents of accounts

The contents of all three main forms of accounts are basically the same and in their most simple format include two separate financial statements:

~ the balance sheet

~ the profit and loss account.

The balance sheet is prepared as at the final day of your accounting period and so only represents the position at that time. The actual figures will have fluctuated throughout the year as the business makes sales and purchases. There are three main headings in the balance sheet:

~ assets

~ liabilities

~ capital.

Chapter Two looks at these subjects in greater detail and gives you detailed advice on how to construct your own balance sheet.

The profit and loss account covers all of your trading activity for the accounting period in question, usually 12 months. This period may vary, however, usually in the first year of trading, not only to take account of the requirements of the Inland Revenue but also to make your tax return easier to prepare.

The profit and loss account will summarise all of your sales turnover, together with your expenses and overheads. It will, of course, also give details of your profit or loss for the period. Chapter Three looks at the profit and loss account in greater detail and shows you how to construct your own profit and loss account.

Summary points

★ Do not be put off from preparing your own accounts. They may not meet official accounting standards but they will give you important management information.

★ You must have total control over your business, and management accounts are an essential constituent of this. Get used to preparing them from the outset and they will soon become simple to compile.

★ If you operate as a limited company you must have an accounting system. It is a legal requirement under the various Companies Acts.

2 Understanding Balance Sheets

A balance sheet provides a snapshot of your business. The essential point to remember is that it must balance.

In this chapter six things that really matter:
- ~ Fixed assets
- ~ Current assets
- ~ Current liabilities
- ~ Long-term liabilities
- ~ Capital
- ~ Constructing your balance sheet

B alance sheets are compiled as at the close of business on a defined day and therefore will only represent the position of your business at that time. The assets and liabilities will fluctuate as you trade on a day-to-day basis.

The balance sheet represents all the things that you own (your assets) deducted by all that you owe (your liabilities). This will then provide you with the net worth of your business – your capital stake. It really is as simple as that.

There is nothing mystical about a balance sheet. It is a straightforward document giving a factual financial description of the value of your business. The assets and liabilities will also balance. Even if you have no outside liabilities, your business will still owe you the money initially invested, plus or minus the profits or losses that you have made. A solvent business means that it owes you money. An insolvent business means that you owe it money.*

Is this you?

I don't understand all these financial terms, how can I tell where to put anything in my balance sheet? • Why should one transaction involve two entries in my books? All this appears to do is duplicate everything. • I really cannot see the benefits of spending time trying to construct my own balance sheet.

* *The key to entrepreneurial success is to maintain a solvent business.*

Fixed assets

Fixed assets are assets that are used in running or operating the business and which remain in the business on an ongoing basis. They are usually categorised into sub-headings, examples of which are:

~ land and buildings

~ plant and equipment

~ fixtures and fittings

~ vehicles.

These assets are valued in the balance sheet at cost price less any depreciation as appropriate. Fixed assets, apart from land and buildings, will only have a certain useful life and therefore their value is depreciated or written down on a predetermined basis. This is something that your accountant will advise on and once a formula has been agreed you can also use this in your management accounts.

As examples you may consider that your plant and equipment have a useful life of ten years. You would therefore reduce their value in the balance sheet by 10% of the original cost per annum and charge the cost, i.e. depreciation, to your profit and loss account. This is not a difficult exercise once you have agreed the formula. It is, in fact, the only hypothetical adjustment that you will need to make to all the figures within your accounts. For an example, please see the section on constructing your own balance sheet at the end of this chapter.

There is one other type of fixed asset that you may see in a balance sheet – goodwill. This is classed as an intangible asset because it represents something that has only a hypothetical value.

Current assets

Current assets are assets that are used in the day-to-day operation of your business. They are also known as liquid assets, representing the fact that they are capable of being quickly liquidated into cash. Examples of current assets are:

~ Stock and work in progress – the products

that you hold ready for sale and for a manufacturing company the raw materials and part-finished goods within the production line.

~ Debtors – money that is owed to you by customers to whom you have sold products and allowed them time to pay you. It could also include pre-payments – money that you have paid to someone in advance.

~ Cash in hand and in the bank – money that you hold together with the balances of all bank or other similar accounts. Note that these only include credit balances. If you have a bank overdraft or loan these are not assets but liabilities.

Current assets usually move in a cycle. Cash is invested in stock, the stock is then sold to customers who become debtors. When the customers pay for the products this enables the cycle to start again.

From this you can see the importance of maintaining good control over your debtors. Until they pay you the cycle cannot continue

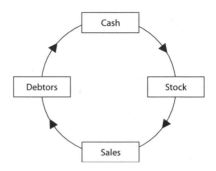

and you may be unable to invest in further stock. This is the downfall of many businesses that generate excellent sales figures but cannot get their customers to pay for the goods.*

Current liabilities

These represent debts that you have which are payable within the next 12-month period. Examples of current liabilities include:

~ Bank balances – the money that you owe your bank on a short-term overdraft basis. If you also have a bank loan, the portion that is payable within the next 12 months should also be included. The balance of the

* Until you actually receive the cash you have not made any profit.

loan payable after the 12-month period will be included as a long-term liability.

~ Creditors – these are usually broken down into sub-headings to cover trade creditors, accruals, and preferential creditors. Trade creditors are suppliers you owe money to. Accruals represent debts that you have which have become due for payment but which have not yet been paid. For example, wages or salaries that are due to your staff but not yet paid. Preferential creditors are the Inland Revenue or HM Customs and Excise. Money due could be for tax, VAT, or National Insurance.

~ Hire purchase or leasing – money that you owe in respect of assets which you have purchased that are being paid for in instalments. Only the amount due within the next 12 months will be included here in exactly the same way as the bank loan.

Once again, the generation of cash is an important aspect when looking at current liabilities. In business, you must always have sufficient cash to meet your liabilities when they fall due, or you will not be in business for very long.

Long-term liabilities

These represent debts that you have that are not due for payment within the next 12 months, but are due for payment after that time. Examples of long-term liabilities include:

~ mortgages or loans

~ hire purchase or leasing.

Only the amount payable after 12 months will be included. The portion payable within the next 12 months has already been accounted for under short-term liabilities.

Capital

This represents the owner's stake in the business, and depending on the legal status of the business – i.e. whether it operates as a limited company, sole trader or partnership – can be shown in two different formats:

~ Limited company – called up share capital. This could also be split to cover the different types of shares, i.e. ordinary or preference shares.

~ Sole trader or partnership – capital account showing the amount initially invested by the owners of the business.

There are also a number of other items that will appear under capital. These could include:

~ revaluation reserves

~ general reserves.

The important thing to remember is that it must balance. To ensure that this happens there must always be two entries for every single transaction. For example, when you buy stock, your stock value increases and your cash balance decreases.

The other important component of capital is the balance of the profit and loss account, which is looked at in Chapter Three.

Constructing your balance sheet

Having looked at the general components of a balance sheet, you can now use this information to construct a balance sheet for your own business. Balance sheets can be set out in either a horizontal or vertical format.*

When making entries in your balance sheet you have only four options for each double entry:

~ Increase an asset – decrease another asset or increase a liability.

~ Decrease an asset – increase another asset or decrease a liability.

~ Increase a liability – decrease another liability or increase an asset.

~ Decrease a liability – increase another liability or decrease an asset.

Assuming that this is your first day in business you can construct an opening balance sheet that will probably look something like this.

ASSETS	LIABILITIES
Cash at Bank £10,000	Owner's Capital £10,000

It is possible that you may also be introducing other assets into your business that you already own, for example tools and equipment together with a motor vehicle. If this is the case you will need to consult an accountant to confirm that your valuation of these assets conforms to both accounting standards and Inland Revenue requirements.

To start your business you use some of the cash to purchase goods from a supplier that you propose to sell to your own customers in due course. Remembering the double entry system, your balance sheet will then look like this.

ASSETS		LIABILITIES	
Stock	£5,000		
Cash at Bank	£5,000	Owner's Capital	£10,000
Totals	£10,000		£10,000

Using the rules set out above you have increased an asset, stock, for which you have paid cash, thereby decreasing another asset. If you had gained the goods on credit, instead of decreasing cash you would have increased a liability in the form of trade creditors. This would have produced the following balance sheet:

ASSETS		LIABILTIES	
Stock	£5,000	Trade Creditors	£5,000
Cash at Bank	£10,000	Owner's Capital	£10,000
Totals	£15,000		£15,000

Having acquired your opening stock, you now sell £2,000 worth of goods for £2,500. This is split between cash sales of £1,500 and sales on credit of £1,000 which is to be paid for by your customers in 30 days' time. Returning to the original format of your balance sheet, where you paid cash for your stock, it will now change to look like this.

ASSETS		LIABILITIES	
Stock	£3,000		
Debtors	£1,000	Owner's Capital	£10,000
Cash at Bank	£6,500	Profit & Loss	£500
Totals	£10,500		£10,500

At this stage you can see that a new entry, profit, has been added to the liabilities side of your balance sheet. Chapter Three gives a detailed description of how your profit and loss account is constructed. For the time being, however, all expenses related to the business are being ignored. In simple terms you can see how this figure of £500 has been calculated. You have sold goods for £2,500 that originally cost you £2,000. In practical terms, the double entry for expenses will relate to cash on the asset side and the profit and loss account on the side of liabilities.

Over the next month you purchase further stock to a value of £20,000, only this time your supplier has granted you credit terms. This allows you to pay for £10,000 worth of the goods after 30 days, with £10,000 being paid in cash. You sell goods for £25,000 – the cost price being £20,000 – and once again your sales are split with £15,000 in cash and £10,000 being payable by your customers in 30 days. The goods that you previously sold on credit for £1,000 have now been paid for by your customers. You have also invested in a motor vehicle costing £5,000, obtaining hire purchase funding of £4,000 towards the cost. In recognition of your efforts in the business you have paid yourself the sum of £1,000.

All of these transactions will mean the following double entries to your balance sheet:

~ Stock value increases by £20,000. Trade creditors increase by £10,000 and cash decreases by £10,000.

~ Sales increase by £25,000, stock decreases by £20,000 and therefore profit increases by £5,000. Cash increases by £15,000 and debtors increase by £10,000.

~ Debtors decrease by £1,000 and cash increases by £1,000.

~ Motor vehicles increase by £5,000 with hire purchase increasing by £4,000 and cash decreasing by £1,000.

~ Your wages reduce profit by £1,000 and cash by £1,000.

Your balance sheet will now look like this:

ASSETS		LIABILITIES	
Motor Vehicle	£5,000	Hire Purchase	£4,000
Stock	£3,000	Trade Creditors	£10,000
Debtors	£10,000	Owner's Capital	£10,000
Cash at Bank	£10,500	Profit & Loss	£4,500
Totals	£28,500		£28,500

If you followed these entries through closely, working from the previous balance sheet to the one above, you will have noticed that cash at one stage was a negative figure. This was, of course, on the basis that your whole trading for the month was entered in your books in one go. Had the balance sheet been worked on a daily basis, buying and selling stock to meet demand and receiving and paying out cash, this would not have happened.

You will also note that an apparent profit has been made of £4,500, although at this stage it is only a book entry. You have still to collect the cash of £10,000 from your debtors and, until this has been received, your profit is only hypothetical.*

Let us now assume that you have been trading for a full year, with sales continuing at virtually the same level as you achieved in your first month. Your balance sheet may now look something like this:

ASSETS		LIABILITIES	
Motor Vehicle	£5,000	Hire Purchase	£3,000
Stock	£6,000	Trade Creditors	£13,000
Debtors	£15,000	Owner's Capital	£10,000
Cash at Bank	£20,500	Profit & Loss	£20,500
Totals	£46,500		£46,500

* If, for example, half of your debtors default on payment, your profit of £4,500 will turn into a real loss of £500.

In order to present this information in a final version of your balance sheet, you need to consider a number of factors. The value of the motor vehicle after 12 months will not be the same as the cost price. You now need to depreciate this asset to reflect its real value in the business. Noting that hire purchase has reduced by 25%, in other words you have contracted to pay for the motor vehicle over four years, it is not unreasonable to depreciate the asset by the same relative amount.

The value of the motor vehicle therefore needs to be depreciated, or written down, by 25% and the cost passed to your profit and loss account. This reduces the value of the vehicle in the balance sheet to £3,750, with the resultant reduction of £1,250 being taken from profits.

You also need to remember that part of the hire purchase debt is a short-term liability, payable within 12 months, and the balance is a long-term liability, payable after 12 months. Only the capital element of the debt is shown in the balance sheet, interest on the debt is dealt with separately in the profit and loss account.

In order to present all of this figure information to a format normally employed by accountants, your balance sheet will now be transformed to look like this:

Fixed Assets		
Motor Vehicle	£5,000	
less Depreciation	£1,250	
		£3,750
Current Assets		
Stock	£6,000	
Debtors	£15,000	
Cash at Bank	£20,500	
Total Current Assets	£41,500	
Current Liabilities		
Hire Purchase	£1,000	
Trade Creditors	£13,000	
Total Current Liabilities	£14,000	
Net Current Assets		
(£41,500 − £14,000)		£27,500
Long-term Liabilities		
Hire Purchase	£2,000	
Total Net Assets		
(£3,750 + £27,500 − £2,000)		£29,250

Represented by:
Capital Account   £10,000
Profit and Loss Account
(£20,500 − £1,250)   £19,250
                                       £29,250

Constructing your own balance sheet is not difficult. The key points to remember are to make all entries one at a time and make sure that the figures still balance after you make any changes. This makes finding errors a lot easier.*

Always be logical in your approach. Remember that all the entries relate to a transfer of something into or out of your business. For example, the purchase of stock involves the transfer into your business of an asset and the transfer out of your business of another asset, cash. You have effectively exchanged one item in the balance sheet for another.

* *Think about the changes you are going to make before you make them and decide which of the four basic options described earlier in this chapter will apply.*

Summary points

★ Make sure you understand the difference between an asset and a liability.

★ Do not be afraid of constructing your balance sheet, it is not something that needs to be left to your accountant.

★ Remember that you only have four options when making changes to your balance sheet.

★ Take care with each double entry and ensure that after each change your balance sheet still balances.

3 Understanding a Profit and Loss Account

Profit is the surplus of income minus expenditure. If you don't make a profit you won't be in business for very long.

In this chapter six things that really matter:
~ Sales
~ Cost of sales
~ Gross profit
~ Overheads
~ Net profit
~ Constructing your own profit and loss account

Being in business is all about making a profit. If you leave the preparation of a profit and loss account until after your year end and then find that your expenditure has exceeded your income, i.e. you have made a loss, it is too late to do anything about it.

The preparation of your profit and loss account on a regular basis is therefore crucial.

It should be prepared at least monthly, with the actual figures compared with your budgeted figures. You can then quickly take steps to put your performance back on track if there is any variance.

The two key pieces of information that you will gain from your profit and loss account are first that you are reaching, or exceeding your sales targets and second that you are keeping tight control over your costs. These are essential activities if you are to ensure that you make a profit.[x]

Is this you?

Why should I bother with a profit and loss account – if I've got money in the bank I must be making a profit. • Why should I calculate the cost of sales and undertake a stock check, I'll just use the cost of the goods that I've bought. • It would be a lot easier to just add all my expenses together, why should I try and itemise them into headings?

* Profitability is the most important part of your business. Without profits you are gaining no return on your investment in terms of both time and money.

Sales

Sales take two forms, either paid for in cash or granted on credit terms. In other words, your sales are either paid for immediately or at some later date which has been agreed between you and the purchaser. At this stage it is important that you understand how to calculate your sales figures for a defined period.

If you are only dealing in cash sales then it is simply the amount of cash that you have received in the period. If, however, you make sales on credit terms you must include the value of the goods or services delivered and not just the cash received. Sales have still been made even though you have not actually received payment for them.

Another important aspect is that if you are registered for Value Added Tax (VAT) then you must exclude the VAT element from all of the figures in your accounts. The reason for this is quite simple, it is not your money.

From your sales figures you must also deduct the value of any goods returned to you by your customers for any reason. You must also deduct any discounts that you have allowed. This will then give you your true sales figure for the period.

Cost of sales

The cost of sales will vary with your sales volume. If you are buying and selling goods, either on a retail or wholesale basis, the cost of sales will equal the cost of the goods sold. Note that it is not the cost of the goods that you have bought. Some of these goods are probably still held as stock.

The cost of sales in this case is calculated by taking your stock valuation as at the start of the period, adding the cost of the goods bought, then deducting the value of the stock held at the end of the period. As an example, at 1 January you held £5,000 worth of stock. During the month you purchased stock worth £35,000. At 1 February your stock holding was £7,000. Cost of goods sold therefore equates to:

Opening stock	£5,000
plus purchases	£35,000
	£40,000
less closing stock	£7,000
Cost of goods sold	£33,000

An important point to remember when looking at stock valuations is that you must always use the actual cost of the goods. You must not use the selling price. Obviously you should also have a system in place to assess accurately the value of your stock on an ongoing basis.

Cost of sales is calculated in a different way if your business is involved in manufacturing. In this case you are taking raw materials and turning them into a finished product that is then sold. Your cost of sales must, therefore, also include the direct costs of production and not just the cost of the raw materials. In this case you would then include the wages of those workers directly involved in making the finished product.

Another example is where you employ staff whose time you effectively sell, for example in a car repair workshop. In this case your cost of sales, apart from the replacement parts, would be mostly the wages costs of the employees. Remember, however, that they must be direct costs. The wages of the office administrator, who makes no contribution to actually making or repairing anything, would not be included in your cost of sales. These would be included later in your overheads.

Gross profit

The gross profit, or gross margin as it is sometimes called, is now easily calculated. You merely take the sales figure and deduct the cost of sales to arrive at the gross profit. Gross profit is extremely important. It must be sufficient to cover all the overhead expenses of running your business, otherwise you are trading at an overall loss.

For this reason it is now appropriate to consider the gross profit in relation to the break-even sales level. The break-even point is where you just make sufficient gross profit to cover your overheads. As an example, your overhead costs amount to £10,000 per annum and the gross profit percentage amounts to 10%. Just to break even you must achieve sales of £100,000 per annum.*

Overheads

Also referred to as fixed costs, overheads relate to all the other expenses of running your business. These will not tend to vary with the costs of production and will remain fairly constant over time. Examples of overheads include:

~ rent and rates

~ heating, lighting and water

~ telephone, stationery and postage

~ advertising and promotion.

Whilst it is easy to identify all the overheads relating to your business – they are all the expenses that have not been attributed elsewhere – there is one extremely important point to consider. The overhead cost must relate to the accounting period in question. As an example, you pay your rent

* *Break-even point is a term that is very important to all businesses. Most business owners, however, have no idea what their break-even point is. Without this information you cannot take action, either to reduce costs or to try to increase your gross profit margin should your sales fall below this figure.*

quarterly in advance in March, June, etc., but the accounting period you are looking at is only for March.

This means that only a third of the rent will be included in your overhead cost, the other two-thirds will appear in your balance sheet as a prepayment. It is money paid in advance and therefore an asset within the business. The same will apply in reverse for overheads that are paid in arrears, for example your telephone bill.

You may need to make an estimate of the amount that will be payable in due course and include this in your overheads. You will also need to show this entry in your balance sheet as a liability. It is money that is owed by you even though you have not as yet received a bill.*

* *Overheads are the expenses that are due within the accounting period in question. They are not just those that have been physically paid for during that period.*

Net profit

Net profit is calculated by deducting the overhead costs from your gross profit. At this stage it also excludes any drawings made by the owners of the business, any payments to shareholders in the case of a limited company, and taxation. These payments are usually shown at the bottom of the profit and loss account in a separate appropriation account.

Net profit is obviously of prime importance to you. Even after taking sufficient drawings for yourself there should still be profit left in the profit and loss account to increase the net worth of your business and provide for future investment. If you do not make a net profit you will gain nothing from being in business. This means that you are gaining no reward for the extra effort required to run your own business. In simple terms, you might be better off selling the business, investing the money and finding a job on an equivalent salary. At least that way you will be gaining a return on your investment.

This is something that many small-business owners do not appreciate. Whilst the business is providing them with an acceptable income they are happy. Only when they come to retire do they realise that with no retained profits in the business, it cannot be sold to provide them with a sizeable lump sum. Unless they have invested in a private pension all they are left with is their original investment which, with inflation, is probably now minimal. They are then faced with the prospect of having to carry on working to gain an acceptable income.

Constructing your own profit and loss account

In constructing your own profit and loss account you are merely summarising all of your income and all of your expenditure. The important thing to remember is to keep it simple. Do not allocate every different type of expense to a different heading. For example, it is quite acceptable to summarise in one heading all of your expenditure on heating, lighting and power.

The easiest way to construct your profit and loss account is to do it in two stages:

~ the calculation of your gross profit

~ the calculation of your net profit.

For the first part of your profit and loss account you will need the total figure for sales made in the period and the cost of those sales. This will then reveal your gross profit for the period in question. There are many different ways you can set out this information, but I would suggest that you organise your figures in a vertical format. This means that the initial part of your profit and loss account will look something like this:

Profit and Loss Account for the three months ending 31 December

Total Sales		£57,481
Opening Stock – as at 1 October	£17,534	
plus Purchases	£35,667	
SUB TOTAL	£53,201	
less Closing Stock – as at 31 December	£18,275	
		£34,926
Gross Profit		£22,555

If you have other expenses that can be directly attributed to your cost of sales these would be included in the first section of your profit and loss account. These might, for example, include wages for production workers and they would be itemised below your stock calculation.

The next stage in the construction of your profit and loss account is to summarise all of your overhead expenses. By deducting these from the figure you have already calculated for your gross profit you will reveal your net profit for the period. As stated above, you can organise your expenses under different groups and provide an overall total instead of separate figures.

Once you have established your appropriate account headings you should keep them the same, with the same expenses being allocated to the same headings on a consistent basis. This will make it a lot easier for you to make a comparison at a later date, thereby improving your financial analysis when assessing your costs.

The second part of your profit and loss account may therefore look something like the one shown overleaf:

Gross Profit brought forward:		£22,555
Staff Wages and National Insurance	£6,600	
Rent and Rates	£1,976	
Insurance	£765	
Light, Heat and Power	£968	
Repairs and Renewals	£443	
Motor and Travel	£1,893	
Legal and Professional	£200	
Accountancy	£150	
Printing, Stationery and Postage	£548	
Advertising	£760	
Telephone	£186	
Training	£450	
Cleaning	£600	
Bank Interest	£12	
Bank Charges	£68	
Bad Debts	£137	
Depreciation	£960	
		£16,716
Net Profit		£5,839

This is not a definitive list of all the headings that you may wish to consider. It merely demonstrates the type of headings that are commonly used. You should use whatever headings will best suit your business.

Summary points

★ Do not include VAT in any of your figures – this money does not belong to your business, it belongs to the government.

★ Make sure you correctly calculate your cost of sales, it is not the cost of goods purchased.

★ Calculate the break-even point for your business and ensure that your gross profit is sufficient to cover your overheads.

★ Classify your overheads into appropriate headings and then allocate the same expenses to the same headings on a consistent basis.

★ When constructing your profit and loss account, keep it simple, but accurate.

4 Understanding a Cash Flow Forecast

Run out of cash and your business will more than likely fail. You must plan the flow of cash into and out of your business.

In this chapter four things that really matter:
~ What are they used for?
~ How are they constructed?
~ Why bother with them at all?
~ Specimen cash flow forecast

Cash is like the flow of blood through your veins. If the flow stops you will die. In the same way, if the flow of cash into your business ceases, your business will not survive. Long-term and short-term cash flow planning are essential components of your business planning activities. In many cases a cash flow forecast is prepared too late and for the wrong reason, usually at the request of the bank to assess your request to borrow money.

Cash flow forecasts must be prepared on a realistic basis – probably the minimum sales and the maximum expenses that you consider likely. This will give you the worst case scenario. It is far better at a later date to present your bank with actual sales figures that have exceeded the forecasts and expenses that are less than forecast.*

* All too often I have received telephone calls from business owners seeking funding to pay one bill or another due to a shortage of cash. They had really left it far too late to seek assistance. If they had taken the trouble to complete a cash flow forecast they would have recognised the potential problem well in advance.

Is this you?

How can I prepare a cash flow forecast when I have no idea what my sales will be? • I don't need to forecast cash flow, making sales is more important to me. • The bank did ask me for a cash flow forecast when I started the business, but I haven't used it since.

What are they used for?

A cash flow forecast is used to forecast the cash that will flow into and out of your business. It is not concerned with anything other than cash and will therefore not indicate whether you are making profits or losses. It is a vital tool in controlling your business to ensure that liquidity is maintained.

Liquidity, in terms of actual cash, is essential to all businesses no matter what their size. Orders from customers are of no value whatsoever if you do not have the funds to manufacture the goods. In the same way, a warehouse full of stock will not pay the wages unless the goods can be sold and thereby converted into cash.

Understanding, and indeed controlling, how the cash flows through your business is one of the most important management issues that you must address. In simple terms, cash flows through your business as shown opposite.

From this simple diagram you can see that if any part of the process is disrupted, for example through late or non-payment by your customers, then you are likely to encounter a shortage of cash. Planning for such disruptions in cash flow will give you

greater control over your financial stability and, in the long run, the whole viability of your business.*

How are they constructed?

The construction of a cash flow forecast is relatively simple. All you need to do is estimate the cash flowing into and out of your business. If you have been trading for some time this is made even easier because you can, of course, base your estimates on previous actual figures. For an example of a completed cash flow forecast please refer to the final section of this chapter.

The forecast has been prepared on the basis that this is a new start business and consequently there is no opening bank balance. The expenditure is broken down into a number of components and whilst it does not really matter how many of these you have it is important that you remain consistent with your headings. This will make it a lot easier to monitor your expenditure and gives you the ability to make direct comparisons between historic figures and forecast figures. It will also provide you with some basic tools to analyse the relationship between sets of figures, for example, the costs of advertising compared to the sales generated.

It is important that your basic assumptions regarding the time that you will allow your customers to pay you and the time that your suppliers will allow you to pay them are accurate. Remember that these are forecasts. It is infinitely preferable that your actual figures are better than expected rather than worse. It can be difficult to explain to your bank why your sales figures are less than anticipated and/or your costs are greater than forecast. If your forecasts can be seen to be accurate the bank will have greater confidence in your ability, not only to run your business, but also to control your finances.

It is relatively easy to project your expenditure because you should be able to accurately assess your overhead costs. Projecting your income can, however, be much more difficult, especially if you are constructing the forecast for a new business. In this case it is essential that your market research into sales potential is accurate in order to ensure that your forecasts are realistic.

Why bother with them at all?

Quite often businesses prepare cash flow forecasts for totally the wrong reason. Usually this is at the insistence of their bank whom they have approached for funding at a time when the flow of cash has dwindled and is insufficient to cover expenditure. By this time their own initial cash injection has been totally eroded and effectively they no longer have any investment in the business. It is for this reason that the bank will more than likely decline the request because the business has shown a lack of forward planning and lost control of its finances.

If such businesses had used a cash flow forecast as part of their overall business planning they would have recognised that further funding might be required to bridge the funds expected from their customers. Consider the following scenario:

You start your own business and formulate a cash flow forecast that uses the assumptions that you will allow your customers 30 days to pay you for goods and your own suppliers will also allow you 30 days to pay them. You estimate that the overhead costs of running the business will be £1,500 per month and that you will sell goods to the value of £7,500 per month which actually cost you £5,000 to purchase. As opening capital you inject all of your savings of £2,500, which will more than cover the first month's trading pending receipt of funds from your customers.

Under these circumstances, in simple terms, your cash flow forecast for the first five months' trading will looking something like this:

Receipts	Month 1	Month 2	Month 3	Month 4	Month 5
Capital Investment	£2,500				
Cash from Customers		£7,500	£7,500	£7,500	£7,500
Payments to Suppliers		£5,000	£5,000	£5,000	£5,000
Expenses	£1,500	£1,500	£1,500	£1,500	£1,500
Net Cash Flow	£1,000	£1,000	£1,000	£1,000	£1,000
Opening Bank		£1,000	£2,000	£3,000	£4,000
Closing Bank	£1,000	£2,000	£3,000	£4,000	£5,000

This looks a very satisfactory situation provided the assumptions are correct. What happens, however, if only a third of your customers pay you on time with the remaining two-thirds paying you after 60 days? The forecast then looks like this:

Receipts	Month 1	Month 2	Month 3	Month 4	Month 5
Capital Investment	£2,500				
Cash from Customers		£2,500	£7,500	£7,500	£7,500
Payments to Suppliers		£5,000	£5,000	£5,000	£5,000
Expenses	£1,500	£1,500	£1,500	£1,500	£1,500
Net Cash Flow	£1,000	(£4,000)	£1,000	£1,000	£1,000
Opening Bank		£1,000	(£3,000)	(£2,000)	(£1,000)
Closing Bank	£1,000	(£3,000)	(£2,000)	(£1,000)	£0

Whilst this late payment only affected one figure in the first month of the forecast it has meant that unless you can obtain further funding to support the business over the first five months it is unlikely to survive after the first month's trading. This exercise should demonstrate to you the importance of accurate forecasting. If this is absent it is very easy for a business to fail.*

* Having completed the forecasts it is essential that you compare your actual financial performance against the budgeted figures. This will enable you to update your forecasts and give you prior warning of any potential liquidity problems in the future.

In summary, the preparation of a cash flow forecast will assist your business planning in four key areas:

~ It will help you to ensure that adequate cash is available to meet the needs of your business.

~ You will be able to assess whether you will have sufficient cash for future capital expenditure.

~ By forecasting accurately you will be able to manage your cash resources, enabling interest charges on borrowed money to be minimised and surplus funds to be invested on a short-term basis.

~ It will enable you to identify any short-term cash shortage and raise suitable funds in advance to avoid a cash crisis.

Specimen cash flow forecast

In drawing up this cash flow forecast, the following assumptions were made:

~ Sales receipts – 50% in cash
                 – 25% after 30 days
                 – 25% after 60 days.

~ Bank loan of £30,000 is repayable over 10 years with interest fixed at 7.5%.

~ Grants will be received equating to 5% of capital expenditure.

	January	February	March	April	May	June
SALES						
Product 1	4,000	5,500	6,500	7,500	7,500	7,500
Product 2	2,000	3,500	5,500	5,500	6,500	6,500
Product 3	2,000	3,500	5,000	5,000	5,000	8,000
TOTAL	8,000	12,500	17,000	18,000	19,000	22,000
RECEIPTS						
Debtors	4,000	8,250	13,625	16,375	18,250	20,250
Owners	40,000					
Grants	2,000			250		
Loans	30,000					
Other						
VAT	700	1,444	2,384	2,866	3,194	3,544
TOTAL	76,700	9,694	16,009	19,491	21,444	23,794
PAYMENTS						
Raw Materials	2,800	4,375	5,950	6,300	6,650	7,700
Wages & NI	3,500	3,500	3,500	3,500	3,500	3,500
Rent	1,200	1,200	1,200	1,200	1,200	1,200
Rates	200	200	200	200	200	200
Insurance	1,650			1,650		
HLP	2,000	450			450	
Telephone	650		350			350
Advertising	3,500	500	500	500	500	500
Office costs	465	465	465	465	465	465
Travel, etc.	200	200	200	200	200	200
Professional fees	2,500	500			500	
Repairs	100	100	100	100	100	100
Other	100	100	100	100	100	100
Capital	40,000			5,000		
Bank charges	850	150			150	
Loan repayments	250	250	250	250	250	250
Interest	150	150	150	150	150	150
Drawings	1,500	1,500	1,500	1,500	1,500	1,500
Tax						
VAT	9,155	1,171	1,341	2,216	1,569	1,648
VAT to C & E	0			(7,139)		
TOTAL	70,770	14,811	15,806	16,192	17,484	17,863
BALANCE	5,930	(5,117)	203	3,298	3,960	5,931
BANK BALANCE	5,930	813	1,016	4,314	8,274	14,205

July	August	September	October	November	December	TOTAL
85,00	8,500	8,000	8,000	6,500	6,500	84,500
7,000	7,000	7,000	6,500	6,500	6,000	69,500
8,000	8,000	5,000	5,000	5,000	5,000	64,500
23,500	23,500	20,000	19,500	18,000	17,500	218,500
22,000	23,125	21,750	20,625	18,875	18,125	205,250
						40,000
250			250			2,750
						30,000
						0
3,850	4,047	3,806	3,609	3,303	3,172	35,919
26,100	27,172	25,556	24,484	22,178	21,297	313,919
8,225	8,225	7,000	6,825	6,300	6,125	76,475
3,500	3,500	3,500	3,500	3,500	3,500	42,000
1,200	1,200	1,200	1,200	1,200	1,200	14,400
200	200	200	200	200	200	2,400
1,650			1,650			6,600
	450			450		3,800
		350			350	2,050
500	500	500	500	500	500	9,000
465	465	465	465	465	465	5,580
200	200	200	200	200	200	2,400
	500			500	250	4,750
100	100	100	100	100	100	1,200
100	100	100	100	100	100	1,200
5,000			5,000			55,000
	150			150		1,450
250	250	250	250	250	250	3,000
150	150	150	150	150	150	1,800
1,500	1,500	1,500	1,500	1,500	1,500	18,000
						0
2,553	1,845	1,525	2,308	1,508	1,416	28,255
4,170			5,780			2,811
29,764	19,335	17,040	29,729	17,073	16,306	282,171
(3,664)	7,837	8,516	(5,244)	5,106	4,991	31,748
10,542	18,379	26,895	21,651	26,757	31,748	

~ Raw material costs will equate to 35% of the selling price.

~ Being a new business, no trade credit is available for the first year.

~ VAT is calculated at 17.5%.

Summary points

★ You must compile cash flow forecasts on a regular basis to ensure that your business retains liquidity.

★ Be realistic when you assess the figures.

★ Always review actual performance against the forecasts.

★ Update the forecasts using the actual figures to amend your future projections.

Understanding a Source and Application of Funds Statement

Understanding the actual source and application of funds through your business is just as important as forecasting where it will come from and where it will go.

In this chapter four things that really matter:
~ The difference between funds and cash
~ What does it show?
~ How is it used?
~ Specimen Source and Application of Funds Statement

Unfortunately, the formulation of a Source and Application of Funds Statement is often considered as unnecessary by many small businesses. It is, however, one of the tools for managing your business and can therefore be used to assist with planning the financial resources of your business.

It provides a link between the opening and closing balance sheets and the profit and loss account for the period. As we have already established, the balance sheet only provides a snapshot of the business as at the opening and closing dates and the profit and loss account relates only to income and expenditure.*

Is this you?

My business is not large enough to need this complicated statement. • My accountant usually compiles one of these but I don't understand it. • I don't see the need for one of these, the balance sheet and profit and loss account tell me all I need to know about my business.

The difference between funds and cash

From the outset you must understand the difference between funds, or financial resources, and cash. Just because a business

The Statement of Source and Application of Funds relates to the actual use of funds within the business. This can then be compared with the cash flow forecast prepared previously to aid the formulation of a new cash flow forecast.

shows a profit in the profit and loss account does not mean that such profit is actually held in cash, although it has funded the business. It is more than likely that the cash generated from sales, including the profit element, has already been re-invested in the business. Such investment may be in current assets such as stock which can be used to generate further cash, or fixed assets such as equipment which of course will not generate any cash return unless the asset is sold.

In both cases cash has been used to purchase an asset, effectively exchanging one asset for another, and accordingly the overall financial resources of the business have not changed. The funds remain in the business but the actual hard cash itself has been utilised. The profit shown in the accounts is therefore merely a book-keeping entry and does not mean that such a sum is sitting in a deposit account somewhere ready to be used.

By the same token, consider the depreciation entry in the profit and loss account. This is an allocation of funds as a charge against profits, although it does not involve any movement of cash. It is merely a book-keeping entry to reduce the value of an asset in the balance sheet so that the amount shown reflects the true value of the asset should it have to be sold to generate cash.

Funding for your business may also come from other sources that do not involve cash, for example, creditors that allow you time to pay for your supplies. In the same way you may also provide funds to your customers by allowing them time to pay you for goods they have received from you. Neither of these examples would involve any exchange of cash until either your customers pay for the goods or you pay your creditors.*

* Cash is a source of funds, but not all funds are cash. You must understand the distinction so as to ensure that adequate liquid funds are available to finance your business.

What does it show?

In simple terms, the Source and Application of Funds Statement shows where financial resources have come from and where those funds have been utilised. It provides a link between the balance sheet and profit and loss account to explain the difference between the financial resources of the business at the start of the accounting period and the end of the accounting period.

There are many different formats for preparing and presenting a Source and Application of Funds Statement. Two different examples are given at the end of this chapter. It is, of course, also possible for historic or projected figures to be used. Historic and projected versions would be compiled in exactly the same way, using the same sources for the figure information. Provided you are consistent with the format that you use, it really does not matter how you choose to present the information.

There are five essential components of the Source and Application of Funds Statement:

~ The profit or loss for the period with suitable adjustments for any non-cash items, depreciation being the main example.

~ Details of any dividends paid.

~ Acquisitions or disposals of any fixed assets.

~ Funds raised or repaid relating to external

loans or an increase or decrease in share capital.

~ The increase or decrease in working capital relating to stocks, debtors, creditors and any other current assets or liabilities.

The Source and Application of Funds Statement is not a replacement for the profit and loss account and the balance sheet. The information that it contains is a selection, re-classification and summary of the figures contained in those two financial statements. Accordingly, the Statement does not indicate the capital requirements of the business and, being a snapshot of the financial information, cannot indicate the day-to-day working capital requirements in terms of stocks, debtors or creditors. This information can only be obtained from your cash flow forecast.

How is it used?

The Source and Application of Funds Statement is used to understand where the funding for your business has come from – or for a forecast Statement, where the funding will come from – and exactly where those funds have been used. There are many sources of funds, some of which are not initially readily identifiable. One of the main examples is the use of trade creditors. By allowing you time to pay they are providing your business with a loan. In exactly the same way, as is often misunderstood, application of funds is the money that is owed to you by debtors. By allowing them time to pay you are also granting them a loan.

Remember that you must retain adequate control over your debtors and creditors to ensure that cash is available as and when required to fund your business. Allowing your debtors too long to pay you could mean that you run out of cash – and your creditors may not allow you to delay payment to them purely because of your lack of control.

Completing a Source and Application of Funds Statement will allow you to analyse and reconcile your financial performance. It will also give you an indication of how much reliance you are placing on the forbearance of your creditors, which under no circumstances should be abused. The Statement can also be used in conjunction with ratio analysis, which is explained in Chapter Six. This will ensure that your financial performance is consistent or improving, or allow you to take steps to rectify the position if it is deteriorating.

Specimen Source and Application of Funds Statement

The easiest way to understand how the Source and Application of Funds Statement is used is to look at an actual example. In order to achieve consistency, a profit and loss account and balance sheet are shown below based on the cash flow forecast in Chapter Four. This will give you an understanding of exactly where all the figures have come from.

PROFIT AND LOSS ACCOUNT – YEAR ONE

SALES	£218,500	
less Direct Costs	£54,625	
GROSS PROFIT		£163,875
EXPENDITURE		
Wages & NI	£42,000	
Rent	£14,400	
Rates	£2,400	
Insurance	£6,600	
Heating, Lighting and Power	£3,800	
Telephone	£2,050	
Advertising	£9,000	
Office costs	£5,580	
Travel, etc.	£2,400	
Professional fees	£4,750	
Repairs	£1,200	
Other	£1,200	
Bank charges	£1,450	
Depreciation	£11,000	
TOTAL		(£107,830)
NET PROFIT		£56,045
Other Income – Grant received		£2,750
Interest		(£1,800)
Drawings		(£18,000)
RETAINED IN THE BUSINESS		£38,995

BALANCE SHEET – YEAR ONE

FIXED ASSETS		
Capital Equipment	£55,000	
less Depreciation	£11,000	
		£44,000
CURRENT ASSETS		
Stock	£21,850	
Cash at Bank	£31,748	
Debtors	£13,250	
		£66,848
Current LIABILITIES		
Loans	£27,000	
VAT	£4,853	
		£31,853
NET CURRENT ASSETS		£34,995
NET ASSETS		78,995
FINANCED BY:		
Owner's Capital	£40,000	
Profit & loss	£38,995	
TOTAL		£78,995

SOURCE OF FUNDS

Profit	£54,245
Depreciation added back	£11,000
Funds Generated from Operations	£65,245
Capital Introduced	£40,000
Long-term Loan	£30,000
Grants	£2,750
TOTAL SOURCE OF FUNDS	£137,995

APPLICATION OF FUNDS

Purchase of Fixed Assets	£55,000
Drawings	£18,000
Loan Repayments	£3,000
	£76,000
NET FLOW OF FUNDS	£61,995

WORKING CAPITAL

Stock increase (+) or decrease (−)	£21,850
Debtors increase (+) or decrease (−)	£13,250
Cash/Bank increase (+) or decrease (−)	£31,748
Creditors increase (−) or decrease (+)	−£4,853
NET INCREASE IN FUNDS	£61,995

There are a number of different formats for a Source and Application of Funds Statement, although the above example is the most common. Another format, which uses exactly the same information, is given below. You should specifically note the different way in which the working capital elements, i.e. stock, debtors, creditors and cash, are treated.

Source and Application of Funds

Profit	£54,245
Depreciation added back	£11,000
Funds Generated from Operations	£65,245
Stock increase (–) or decrease (+)	– £21,850
Debtors increase (–) or decrease (+)	– £13,250
Creditors increase (+) or decrease (–)	£4,853
Working Capital Surplus (+) or Deficit (-)	–£30,247
True Funds Generated from Operations	£34,998
Capital Expenditure (–)	–£55,000

Grants received (+)	£2,750
Drawings (−)	−£18,000
Total Funds Generated (+)	
or Absorbed (−)	−£35,252
Financed by:	
Capital Introduced	£40,000
Loan net increase (+) or decrease (−)	£27,000
Cash increase (−) or decrease (+)	−£31,748
Total Source of Finance	£35,252

Summary points

★ Make sure you understand the difference between funds and cash and the different forms that sources and applications of funds can take.

★ Use the Statement to link together your balance sheet and profit and loss account to aid the analysis of your business's financial performance.

★ Keep control of your working capital and understand how changes in stock levels and payment terms for both debtors and creditors will affect your funding requirement.

★ Once you have established a format for your Source and Application of Funds Statement, make sure you keep it consistent to aid future analysis.

Using Ratio Analysis

Ratio analysis can help you understand how your business is performing. Abuse it, however, and it will not assist you at all.

In this chapter five things that really matter:
~ What are ratios?
~ How are they used?
~ Efficiency ratios
~ Liquidity ratios
~ Profitability ratios

Ratio analysis has an important role in business planning but, as with all forms of statistical analysis, there can be many pitfalls in its use. Before attempting to conduct any analysis of your financial performance you must understand how ratios can be used and also be aware of their limitations.

Ratios in isolation, based on one year's trading performance, can mean very little because of the lack of comparable figures. For example, your net profit may equate to 10% of your sales turnover but in isolation the ratio tells you nothing. Is this a good performance or could you do better? Only by comparing this ratio with the same ratio for the next year's trading performance will it actually be of any assistance to you.*

Is this you?

I was never good at maths, this will be far too difficult for me. · It's just playing around with figures. Why should I bother? · I have enough problems understanding my accounts without complicating things further.

What are ratios?

A ratio is a means of comparing one figure with another to create a relationship between the figures. A ratio is always made up of two parts, a numerator and a denominator,

* *Remember the quotation attributed to Disraeli – 'There are three kinds of lies: lies, damned lies, and statistics.' Financial ratios can be extremely useful but they can also be severely misleading if not used correctly.*

although both of these may involve a combination of figures. This will become evident when later in this chapter we look at some of the common ratios used to analyse financial accounts.

The figures used will need to be relevant to each other to ensure that the end ratio actually has some meaning – for example, profit to sales or assets to liabilities. Making a comparison between figures for say, your annual profits and your closing bank balance would give you a ratio that has no purpose.

There are also different ways to calculate some ratios. As with all forms of analysis it sometimes does not matter how you calculate the ratio. The important part is that you remain consistent and use the same comparable figures in exactly the same way. An example of such differences in calculation is given in the later section covering liquidity ratios with the example of stock turnover.*

* *In summary, a ratio is a figure that is produced from at least two other figures to establish the relationship between them. A ratio in isolation provides little information to you about your financial performance. It is merely a means of linking together different parts of your financial accounts.*

How are they used?

Whilst they are a valuable tool for analysis,

ratios are often misused and indeed often misinterpreted. Ratios should be used with caution. You must understand the significance of the ratio before its analysis will provide any benefit to your business.

There are two key uses for ratio analysis:

~ To provide a comparison between two or more variables in your accounts, either as a ratio of one to the other, or expressed as a percentage, or one as a multiple of the other.

~ To compare the results from two or more sets of financial accounts to disclose the trends and relationships between the figures that would not be evident from the figures alone.

Quite apart from using ratios to assess your business performance you can also compare your results with other businesses in the same industry or sector. You could, if you were able, obtain the annual accounts of other similar businesses or you could approach organisations such as the Centre for Interfirm Comparison or ICC Business Publications Ltd who provide specialist reports on industry sectors.*

Efficiency ratios

Efficiency ratios concentrate on your use of funds within the business. They look at the working capital elements within your accounts, i.e. stock, debtors and creditors, and establish just how good you are at controlling your finances. There are many different ways that each ratio can be calculated. For example, the sales to stock ratio can be expressed in at least three ways:

$$\frac{\text{Stock}}{\text{Sales}} = \text{Stock turnover ratio}$$

$$\frac{\text{Sales}}{\text{Stock}} = \text{Number of times stock turned over}$$

$$\frac{\text{Stock} \times 365}{\text{Sales}} = \text{Number of days' sales of stock being held}$$

There are other inherent problems because the components are not valued in the same way. The sales figure is the actual selling price of the stock, but the stock contained in the balance sheet is valued at the lower of

The important thing to remember is that ratios merely take two independent parts of your financial accounts to provide a single figure representing the relationship between the constituent components. Only by comparing the same ratios can any trend or pattern be established in your financial performance.

either cost or net realisable value. Moreover, the stock figure could be inflated or deflated because it only relates to the holding on one day of the year.

It is vital that your analysis remains consistent. It does not really matter which calculation method you use. Whilst there are many different ways of calculating the various ratios, in order to avoid confusion, only one example of the method of calculation for each ratio will be given.

In the case of stocks the most common method is the final example above. This reveals approximately the number of days' stock that is being held, which can vary quite widely depending on your business. If, for example, you sell fresh fruit and vegetables, your stock holding would probably be no more than a few days. On the other hand, if you run a book shop you may find that stock turnover, expressed in days, would be substantially longer.

As with all ratios the important aspect is the trend. An increase in the number of days could indicate that you are holding obsolete or damaged items that are ultimately un-saleable. The ideal position is that you only hold the amount of stock considered necessary at any one time.

The other components of working capital, debtors and creditors, are calculated in the same way as stocks:

$$\frac{\text{Debtors} \times 365}{\text{Sales}} = \text{Time in days it takes you to collect payment from debtors}$$

Ideally, the number of days should equate as closely as possible to your terms of trade. The faster you obtain payment the better because this will have a positive impact upon cash flow. If, however, the trend is showing an increase in the number of days, this will require investigation, as it could be due to some, or all, of the following:

~ inadequate control over invoicing

~ slow payment by debtors who are going unchased

~ potential bad debts

~ market competition forcing an increase in

your terms of trade.

Creditors are calculated in the same way using the formula:

$$\frac{\text{Creditors} \times 365}{\text{Sales}} = \text{Time in days that it takes you to pay your creditors}$$

This ratio will indicate how good you are at paying your creditors on time. It should also be compared to the terms of trade that you have with your suppliers. Any lengthening in the trend, whilst having a positive impact on cash flow, could also indicate problems. It may be that you are having to delay payment to your creditors for exactly that reason, a shortage of cash. This should be investigated because if you are abusing your credit you could find the facility withdrawn, with the subsequent severe impact on your finances.

Liquidity ratios

Liquidity ratios examine the relationship between assets and liabilities. They examine the cycle of funds through the business to ensure that stocks and debtors are turned into cash in order to pay creditors. The first ratio used for this purpose is the current ratio. This is calculated by dividing current assets and current liabilities as follows:

Current Assets
Current Liabilities

For a healthy business the resultant answer should be at least two. This would indicate that you have twice as many current assets as current liabilities and therefore should be able to meet your debts as they fall due. However, this ratio may distort the true liquid position because it assumes that stocks can be readily converted into cash.

This may not be true in practice and therefore a liquidity ratio that excludes stock is also used. Known as the 'acid test ratio', this is calculated as follows:

Cash + Debtors
Current Liabilities

The result ratio in this case should not be less than one. Anything less would indicate that you could have liquidity problems and be unable to meet your debts as they fall due. It could also indicate that profit margins are being reduced or even that losses are being incurred.*

The final liquidity ratio calculates the relationship between the funds within the business that have been borrowed from outside sources as opposed to the funds that are invested from internal sources. In simple terms, this is the debt to equity ratio often referred to as the 'gearing ratio'.

There is often argument about the exact external liabilities to be included in this ratio. Once again, this does not really matter provided you are consistent. It is better to look at the worst case scenario and include all sources of outside borrowing regardless of the term. The equity, or net worth, of the business includes the capital account and retained profits. It is sometimes referred to in the balance sheet as 'surplus resources'. the gearing ratio is therefore calculated as follows:

* *Of all the financial ratios, this could be the most important to you in terms of control. Remember, cash is king. Run out of cash and your business could fail.*

Total Borrowing
Net Worth

It is difficult to give an indication of what constitutes an acceptable gearing ratio. All lenders have their own guidelines which, amongst other factors, depend on the quality of the proposition. In general terms, the amount of borrowed money should not exceed the net worth and therefore the resultant figure should be greater than one.

Profitability ratios

As the name would suggest, profitability ratios examine the trend in your profit margins. Profits can be shown in a variety of different stages within your profit and loss account, although there are two that are commonly used – gross profit and net profit. In all cases, the ratio is calculated as a percentage as follows:

Profits x 100
Sales

The gross profit ratio will vary depending

on what sort of business you operate. A manufacturing business could have a high cost overhead which will mean a higher gross profit margin than perhaps a retailer with a high volume of sales but a very fine margin.

Any declining trend in the gross profit ratio should be investigated because it indicates one or more of the following:

~ Margins could be reducing due to competition in the market.

~ The reduction could be due to increased purchase cost of the goods being sold which cannot be passed on to customers.

~ The pricing strategy could be inadequate.

The net profit ratio represents the funds that are being retained in the business to finance future investment and growth. Variations in this ratio are caused by variations in the gross profit margin and the level of overhead expenses. It should show a steady or increasing trend. A declining trend in the net profit ratio which is not matched by a similar decline in the gross profit ratio indicates an increasing trend in overhead expenses. This would require investigation to establish the source of the increased expenditure to enable cost savings to be made for the future. It may also involve a complete review of pricing strategy where expenses cannot be trimmed.

Summary points

★ Make sure you remain consistent in the way you calculate a particular ratio.

★ Do not use ratios in isolation. Use them to compare performance and establish any trends that may need correction.

★ Use the efficiency and liquidity ratios to monitor your working capital and cash flow.

★ Monitor your profitability carefully and investigate quickly when a declining trend is in evidence.